About the author

Gabriel Fitzmaurice was born in 1952 in the village of Moyvane, County Kerry, where he still lives. He has taught in the local national school, where he is now principal teacher, since 1975. He is the author of more than thirty books, including: collections of poetry in English and in Irish; translations from the Irish; poetry for children; a volume of essays; and collections of songs and ballads. He frequently broadcasts on radio and television on education and the arts.

Praise for I and the Village

'… the best contemporary, traditional, popular poet in English.'

– Ray Olson, *Booklist* (US)

'Gabriel Fitzmaurice's new book offers ballads which are comparable with Burns's for their insights and lyricism'

– James J. McAuley, *The Irish Times*

'[L]ike Kavanagh, [Fitzmaurice] makes his own importance from the habitual. There's a cycle of sonnets that lights up love and memory and the daily miracle of Moyvane in Kerry. One proclaims that "my love will take no bullshit", and neither does Fitzmaurice. This poised, rhythmic performance is pub-full of lore and passion.'

– Mary Shine Thompson, *Sunday Independent*

'[Fitzmaurice] is poetry's answer to J[ohn] B. Keane.'

– Fred Johnston

THE BOGHOLE BOYS

Gabriel Fitzmaurice

Best wishes
Gabriel Fitzmaurice

Marino

Marino Books is an imprint of Mercier Press
Douglas Village, Cork
Email: books@mercierpress.ie
Website: www.mercierpress.ie

Trade enquiries to CMD Distribution
55A Spruce Avenue, Stillorgan Industrial Park
Blackrock, County Dublin
Tel: (01) 294 2560; Fax: (01) 294 2564
E-mail: cmd@columba.ie

ISBN 1 86023 158 6
10 9 8 7 6 5 4 3 2 1

A CIP record for this title is available
from the British Library

Mercier Press receives financial assistance from
the Arts Council/An Chomhairle Ealaíon

Cover painting: detail from *The Boghole Boys* by Brenda Fitzmaurice
(gabren@eircom.net).

Printed in England by J. H. Haynes & Co. Ltd., Sparkford

Contents

Preface

The Boghole Boys. Who are they? At the outset, let me state that the term doesn't have any gender implications. Boghole Boys, like Wren Boys, their saturnalian counterparts of Saint Stephen's Day, can be male or female of any age.

'Bog man' is a pejorative term. I come from the bog. I am a bog man and proud of it. When I coined the term 'Boghole Boys', I was mindful of that peculiarly American take on the Odyssey – namely the film *Oh Brother, Where Art Thou?* Some of the best music on that film is provided by a group called The Soggy Bottom Boys. In my own odyssey through my native environment, physical, emotional and spiritual, I sought to translate The Soggy Bottom Boys, the authentic sound of their backwater, to Moyvane. What would the authentic singers of the bog be called? Why, the Boghole Boys of course.

I have prayed and played and sung and danced and drunk, risen and fallen, with these people. These are the men, women and children I meet every day on the street, in my school, in church and in the pub. They are, in many ways, the forgotten people of the new Ireland. Like Tomás Ó Criomhthain's Blasket Islanders, they are a resilient people who make the best of what they've got. They have their heroes and heroines, their teachers and tricksters, their priests and publicans, their successes and suicides. I seek to give voice to these people.

I presented a series, which I called 'The Boghole Boys', on Radio Kerry in January, February and March 2004. Over ten hour-long programmes, we, men and women of my locality, discussed story and recitation, sport, song and songwriting, exile, religion, poetry, teachers and teaching, the old ways, lore and old-time music, pubs and their contribution to the local community. The entire series was drawn from the north Kerry/west Limerick border country where I live – the home of the 'Listowel writers' and the West Limerick musicians – a very special combination.

The Boghole Boys (and girls) spoke, played and sang themselves on that series. An endangered species, I hope I have represented them faithfully in the following pages.

Gabriel Fitzmaurice
Moyvane, July 2004

Introduction

Nobody who has thought seriously about the matter believes either that poems should always rhyme or that they should never rhyme. Most poets rhyme sometimes; a few always rhyme; fewer still never rhyme. But the only general point is that, whether rhyming, non-rhyming, or sometimes-rhyming, a poet of significance has to have some kind of consistent rhythm and language, so that the reader knows how to read them. A trustworthy poem doesn't rhyme or alliterate or feature any kind of linguistic pattern by accident.

Gabriel Fitzmaurice, as we would expect of an outstandingly successful writer of poetry for children, has a wonderful way with rhyming forms. *The Boghole Boys* is full of sonnets and villanelles and other expert structures. The only danger is that the reader, engrossed by the rhymed stories and impressed by the technical facility with which the stories fall effortlessly into place, might fail to notice the shaping and moral fervour that provide the spine of this volume. The early poems take up where Fitzmaurice's acclaimed predecessor book, *I and the Village*, left off, replacing Chagall with Cézanne:

> I write about my village, show it warts
> And all – I must. But I'm a celebrant …
> ('I rhyme my native village with Cézanne')

There is no greater compliment, and no higher claim, as Fitzmaurice proceeds to recognise that his 'glory is that he has such friends' as his fellow-villagers in Moyvane, the labourers who are needed 'to preserve the status quo', the country boys with their 'short coats' and bare feet, and the Nunan sisters acting Beckett for Fr Tom Hickey. This theme culminates in the haunting 'The Day Christ Came to Moyvane': a wonderfully delicate narrative of a tinker/traveller who visits the poet's house, to be roughly driven off by dog and civic guard. That is the whole story as simply told; only the title suggests a weightier significance in the closing lines:

> And as we talked, the tinker man
> Walked farther away from me.

Because of course Fitzmaurice is a writer of passionate principle and political seriousness. The book ends with three big sequences: 'The Village Schoolmaster' (whose fourteen poems are equivalent to the number of lines in a sonnet, or the number of the Stations of the Cross), 'Keeper of the Story' (the story of Ireland's political emergence from the Troubles around 1920), and 'That's Football' (which salutes some of the great names of Kerry football: O'Connell above all; then Sheehy, Brosnan, MacMahon). The great poem here, 'Munster Football Final, 1924', establishes the uniqueness of Fitzmaurice's credentials. It describes and celebrates the extraordinary occasion when the bitter enemies in the civil war, Con Brosnan and John Joe Sheehy, played together for Kerry. Sheehy's republicans were about to lose the war to Brosnan's Free Staters, so it is

> On Con's safe conduct Sheehy takes the field.
> In an hour the Kerry team will win.
> Sheehy will vanish, on Brosnan's bond again.

It would be hard to imagine an event that encapsulates the seriousness of popular culture better. The line before those I have just quoted is

> For what they love, they both put down the gun.

Fitzmaurice avoids the more obvious and clichéd 'the game they love', using the more weighty claim 'for what they love'. Again, the point is made so lightly and so naturally that we can easily miss it.

To return to the kind of generalisations that I started with: the greatest challenge for contemporary poetry, in an age when in fact people seem well disposed to it, is accessibility. Fitzmaurice tells straightforwardly this great story of Brosnan and Sheehy (the All-Ireland medals of both of them are in different shrines in Kerry, now worshipped by the same celebrants) to state a general truth about what we love. It does not devalue politics to see football as also to be taken seriously – a point which is borne out by the first poem in the sequence 'That's Football', which is written in the form reserved (in Irish poetry in particular) for major topics in poetics and politics: Marvell's 'Horatian Ode on Cromwell's Return from Ireland', Yeats' 'Under Ben Bulben', Auden on the death of Yeats, and Heaney on the death of Brodsky.

> For beauty only will suffice,
> Beauty to infuse our lives:
> No cup, no trophy will redeem
> Victory by ignoble means.
>
> ('At the Ball Game', for Seamus Heaney)

Indeed what these poems suggest is that to those who are capable of taking life and love seriously, and of using such terms without embarrassment, everything is to be taken seriously. In the words of Coleridge's great tribute to Charles Lamb,

> No sound is dissonant which tells of life.

Coleridge's musical metaphor is apt in several ways for these poems. The title-poem spells it out with typical lucidity:

> The Boghole Boys are banjo, box, guitar
> And anyone who cares to play along.

Yet again, the point is not laboured, but it is all the more forceful for that. This is a communal art: expert but not exclusive. These are skilled musicians: 'Their Sunday song's as good as you will get'; but anyone can join in to express community and emotion. It represents Fitzmaurice's art perfectly – as indeed it describes the extraordinary school of writing that flourished in north Kerry throughout the twentieth century: a litany of names like those of the footballers, and with some striking overlaps such as MacMahon, Keane, Walsh, Fitzmaurice.

His place in this tradition justifies the claims that Fitzmaurice insistently makes for his own role as poet: claims which he makes out of dedication and regard for the art rather than any impulse towards self-aggrandisement. In the opening 'Cézanne' poem, the claim is made twice in a Kavanaghesque line repeated verbatim:

> A poet finds genius where he can.

This sense of vocation recurs throughout, and is on very solid ground by the end: solid both in its rootedness and in its achievements here. The variety of those achievements is, again, disguised by the vocal and rhythmic consistency. Some lines stay with you –

> To grow apart is part of being free

(The poem is for the poet's son, John: a line that equals Day Lewis' great statement on the same theme, 'And love is proved in the letting go'). Fitzmaurice echoes the English 1930s poets in other ways, particularly in his refusal to exclude public interests from his coverage; Day Lewis comes to mind again, having written one of his great poems on Sheepdog Trials in Hyde Park. This rather remote comparison is worth making because Fitzmaurice, rooted as he is in north Kerry, is entirely unprovincial, finding genius where he is because it is where he is. The best last word for him is his own chosen term, 'celebrant', whether he is celebrating music or football or painting or friendship. He is the most life-enhancing of writers, and this is his most life-enhancing book yet.

Bernard O'Donoghue
November 2004

In memory of my father and mother,
Jack and Maud Fitzmaurice,
and especially for Brenda, John and Nessa,
with love

I Rhyme my Native Village with Cézanne

I rhyme my native village with Cézanne,
The place I live and represent in art,
A poet finds genius where he can,
The picture that he paints is of his heart.
A child, an adolescent and a man
With a vision that the world couldn't thwart,
And still remaining faithful to my plan,
I write about my village, show it warts
And all – I must. But I'm a celebrant,
Not one whose whole ambition's to distort:
Who would grotesque a village like Moyvane
Is painting false, a sell-out to the smart.
I rhyme my native village with Cézanne.
A poet finds genius where he can.

For Seamus Heaney

Rejoice! Rejoice! A laureate named 'Seamus'!
One of us, a bogman proud and true;
Boghole boys ourselves, now who can blame us
If we raise a glass and sing a song to you?
No longer can some *Punch* paint us subhuman,
No more is 'bog' a term of abuse –
'Bogman' is a name that we can bloom in,
Our native sod fit subject for the muse.
As spalpeens herding cattle conversed in Latin,
As bogmen once in hedge schools wrote in Greek,
No more can we, their flesh and blood, be spat on,
We have found the en-Nobel-ment we seek,
A laureate who digs in boggy ground
Unearthing there the riches that abound.

Spalpeens: farm labourers

The Playman

for Fr Tom Hickey

You took Moyvane, a poor, passed-over place,
And showed the world a village in its grace;
You took Dev's comely lasses, sturdy lads
And walked us through the crossroads. I'm glad
I was alive in your time, growing up
In a village that played Beckett, where every pup
That hung about the Corner House had seen
The Nunans – Collette, Dympna, Gerardine –
Transform themselves, and us, upon the stage.
You rehearsed us in the spirit of the age.
Thanks to you, good Father, we learned to play
Our part in the drama of the day.
You understood your village and released
The poetry within us, playman, priest.

At Fifty

I court the common reader, not the poet –
The kind who browses, likes a damn good read:
Let poets (at least the kind who think they know it
All) ignore me. It's not for them I bleed.
No! The ones who read me are the kind
Who know that they can trust a fellow who
Opens up his heart, his soul, his mind.
Unlike words, they know that blood is true.
Let others write for honour and for fame,
Their precious verses often leave me cold,
They can keep their prizes and acclaim,
All that glisters, in the end's, not gold.
There are times a singer's heart despairs of song.
I open a new vein and carry on.

The Poet Strikes Back

He opes his lips! Let no dog bark!
Sir Oracle, Lit. Crit.,
Descends upon the work of art,
A fly upon a shit.

The shit is good and necessary,
It fertilises land;
What's a fly do? Spreads diseases.
I swat it from my hand.

The Celebrant's a Critic

The celebrant's a critic or he's lost
The soul of his own people in a blind
Elevation of his parish at the cost
Of putting the obnoxious from his mind.
They shit on us, these upstarts who return
To the pubs in which they drank; I know their breed –
They boast to old acquaintance as they burn
With all the ostentation of their greed.
Fuck off with your money as you stand
Buying off misfortune at the bar;
I'm a celebrant and though you shake my hand
And act as if in friendship, this is war.
I stand up for my people, mind them well,
I know your kind, your money. Go to hell.

Poet to Poet

I'm sending this though I don't think I should,
My sheaf of poems – took all my life to write.
I need to know if they're any good.

These little poems contain my sweat and blood;
For years I've kept them hidden out of sight.
I'm sending this though I don't think I should.

You won't offend me if you should conclude
That this old lady's poems don't make it quite.
I need to know if they're any good.

My husband laughs and tells me I delude
Myself, such stuff should never see the light.
I'm sending this though I don't think I should

But it's better to know the worst than brood
So I'm sending them (though in not a little fright).
I need to know if they're any good.

Forgive me if you think that I intrude
But a poet like you will surely see my plight.
I'm sending this though I don't think I should.
I need to know if I'm any good.

On First Looking into Brendan Kennelly's *Poetry My Arse*

There is a poem that can't be told in church,
A poem that sings its truth just as it is,
A poem that pulls the preacher from his perch
As he holds on for dear life to certainties;
A poem that confesses to its sin
But out in public – not in some black box;
A love-cry from the depths to let grace in,
So full of life, an outrage! that it shocks.
Tone it down! the pious cry in mock
Indignation, knowing that, full well,
This show of goodness, this pretence at shock is
The hypocrisy that Christ condemned to hell.
The poem shakes deception from its feet
And leaves to sing itself out in the street.

In Memoriam John B. Keane

New Ireland holds you were of Ireland Past,
An Ireland that was changing as you wrote,
That you didn't move with Ireland that was fast
Changing from the times we took the boat
To be Paddies in an England where we'd slave
For a bedroom and a few pints down the pub;
Ireland of the navvy is in its grave,
We've money now where once we used to sub.
'He didn't move with Ireland': let those who
Follow fashion take thought for today;
As Ireland lost its past, a poet, you knew
The timeless things: you wrote them plot and play.
You didn't move with Ireland. No! you stayed
With the primal heart where all true drama's played.

The Ballad of Rudi Doody

a song

My name is Rudi Doody
From Kildeboodybeg,
I'm one week out from Ireland,
Here in Winnipeg;
I'm off to make me fortune
In a land beyond the sea
But I'll ne'er forget where'er I roam
What me mother said to me.

'Goodbye Rudi Doody,
Off to Winnipeg;
Remember Moody Doody
In Kildeboodybeg;
Write a letter now and then
And send us the few pound –
The more we get, the more we want
Till we're six foot underground.'

Then one day a letter came
From far off Winnipeg
Announcing Rudi Doody
To Kildeboodybeg;
He came all rings and biros,
And boasted in the pub

That he could buy the whole damn place
And give every man the sub.

He spent three weeks in Ireland,
Stood all his mates a round,
Staggered to the butcher shop
For the best of steak in town;
And then, the three weeks over,
He packed his case again,
And the cock crew in the mornin'
As he boarded on the plane.

Meanwhile back in Ireland
In Kildeboodybeg,
His mates all toast this *dacent* man
In far off Winnipeg;
But as the years roll onward,
He comes back less and less
For the kids at home drink with their own –
They don't know who he is.

Goodbye Rudi Doody,
Off to Winnipeg;
Remember Moody Doody
In Kildeboodybeg;
Write a letter now and then
And send us the few pound –

The more we get, the more we want
Till we're six foot underground.

The more we get, the more we want
Till we're six foot underground.

Country Roads

Country roads
All potholes
And chip cartons
On the ditch,
Plastic bottles
On grass margins –
Country roads
Are a bitch.

'Almost heaven ...'
Went the story,
Country life,
Cool, clean, fresh air;
I bought a cottage
In the country,
Spent my weekends
Weaving there

Through country roads
All potholes
And chip cartons
On the ditch,
Plastic bottles
On grass margins –
Country roads
Are a bitch.

All my memories
Of the country
Are from childhood
Which one sees
Through rose-tinted
Lying glasses –
Country roads,
Have a look at these

Country roads
All potholes
And chip cartons
On the ditch,
Plastic bottles
On grass margins –
Country roads
Are a bitch.

I hear a voice in the morning
On the roadside,
A voice that's choked by litter
And no one seems to care;
And driving down the road
I get a feeling that I'd like to be
Anywhere,
Anywhere but on these bloody

Country roads
All potholes
And chip cartons
On the ditch,
Plastic bottles
On grass margins –
Country roads
Are a bitch.

Country roads.

Mairg Nach Fuil 'na Dhubhthuatha

after the Irish of Dáibhí Ó Bruadair
(c. 1625–98)

Oh to be pig-ignorant
With money in the bank
Among these boors and upstarts,
Their tabloid *Daily Wank*.

Oh to be pig-ignorant
Then I wouldn't see
The Sunday Poem passed over
For the strippers on page three.

A Local Murder

They all know the murderer
But there's a worse disgrace –
To be an informer
In your native place.

One summer's day a stranger,
Innocent of this code,
Stops for a drink of water
At a cottage on the road.

Suspicious of the stranger,
Yet country courtesy
Invites him to her kitchen;
They small-talk, he and she,

And, looking out the window,
He admires the view;
When it's time to take his leave of her,
He asks, as one will do,

What that nearby hill is called.
Standing at her door
'As true as God, good man,' she says,
'I never saw it before.'

Labourers

'Unskilled' they called them, artists of the spade,
The shovel, four-pronged-pike, the rake, the *sleán*,
Labourers who worked without a trade,
Looked down upon by their very own.
'Unskilled' they called them, men whose skills they'd need
In meadow, bog and garden, and whose toil
Was undervalued in the grab and greed
Of farmers who laid claim to sod and soil.
'Unskilled' they called them as they do today
Though no one uses now the rake and *sleán*,
They draw their dole topped up with odd job pay
And the government condemns this carry on.
Condemn them, men of wealth, 'twas ever so.
You need them to preserve the status quo.

Sleán: a turf-spade, for cutting peat in the bog

Country Boys

You knew them by their short pants and 'short coats',
That's what they called their jackets (some still do),
Bare feet in fine weather, stony roads,
Country boys who walked for miles to school.
We were 'townies' to their 'country' though in truth
The village where we lived was just a cross –
An enemy is needed in pursuit
Of what we are, a stupid 'them' v. 'us'.
When we went to college in the town
We were 'country boys', it didn't matter that
We'd been 'townies' in our village and that noun
Kept us in our place just as we shat
On the country, being townies, till we found,
Between the town and country, our own ground.

Excommunicated, 1939

Darby was a labourer,
One who slaved all day,
He lived not far from Ballymore
On the road out to Knockray

When times were tough and clergy preached
Against 'keeping company',
When the only sin was sexual
And labourers bent the knee

To all who were above them,
When labourers had to eat
Away from the farmer's table
And not every day brought meat.

Darby was fond of women
And women fond of him,
Women found him handsome,
Strong of mind and limb.

He moved in with the Widow Quille
('A hussy who'd no shame')
And lived with her in Ballymore.
The clergy called their names

From the altar
(The intent's to make them cringe,
But Darby and the widow
Live on in sin).

And so one Sunday morning
Father Quinlivan,
A little tyrant of the fields,
A pompous clergyman

Tells the congregation
Gathered at first mass
That he's going to excommunicate
That blackguard of low class

Who dared defy the clergy,
That he'll blow the candles out.
The congregation trembles –
They know he'll carry out

His threat today in Ballymore,
They look on in fear
As he blows out the candles
And, dressed in all his gear,

Processes through the village,
Proclaims to the whole place

That he's excommunicated
And left to his disgrace

A wretch who dared defy him,
The village cowers in dread –
Excommunication means
Your immortal soul is dead.

But Darby smiles his easy smile
And this is all he'll say –
'I'll go to Knockray next Sunday. I'm not
Excommunicated in Knockray.'

So he goes to mass there, Sundays,
To talk and laugh and pray.

The Day Christ Came to Moyvane

He came to fix umbrellas,
Kettles, basins, pans;
The squad car turned in my yard
And jumped the tinker man –

'What are you doing? What's your name?
Get going out of here';
The tinker man walked down the drive,
My dog snapped at his heels.

But the tinker man was used to dogs,
He just kept walking on,
And as he walked he whistled
And was gone.

The guard was doing his duty –
There had been reports
Of travellers casing houses.
I'd been robbed before,

So I thanked the guard and offered him
A beer, a cup of tea,
And as we talked, the tinker man
Walked farther away from me.

Before the Word 'Fuck' Came to Common Use

Before the word 'fuck' came to common use
(Even toddlers going to playschool know it now),
Before the lid was raised on child abuse,
We said that we were innocent. But how?
We heard the whispers and we went along
Protecting those who were above the law
In a world we eulogise ('knew right from wrong'),
A world nostalgia paints without a flaw.
Before the word 'fuck' came to common use
We were children and our masters ran the show ...
Guilty as condemned, it's no excuse
To plead that in the past we didn't know.
Before the word 'fuck' came to common use
Children mattered less than their abusers.

The Mission Magazines

They're in decline, the *Africa,*
Mission Outlook, The Far East,
The divine word is dying
With its nuns and priests.

This testament to piety,
These little acts of hope
With pictures of the mission lands,
Their saints, an ageing pope

Are in decline like religion
In the disillusioned west,
They leave a void behind them
And our defining quest

For eternal truth and beauty
Is consumed like booze
In headlong self-destruction
We call our right to choose.

They're in decline, these pieties,
Relics of the past
In an age of self-expression
Where nothing's said to last.

How Soon the Experts' Views are Obsolete

How soon the experts' views are obsolete,
The stuff they shoved at us: we had no choice.
No amount of experts can compete
With a life that, fully lived, has found its voice.
The stuff they shoved at us is obsolete
As the stuff they're touting now will also be;
The prophets of the moment soon must meet
The only truth there is in prophecy –
That worlds collapse, that even stars will fall,
The only thing that matters is that we
Find our truth, not something that will pall
In the light of tomorrow's prophecy,
Something to hold on to as we go
Wherever living takes us. We don't know.

On Hearing Johnny Cash's *American Recordings*

The great ones have the courage to believe,
The courage to go naked if so called,
To pare life back to where things don't deceive;
Let those ashamed of feeling be appalled,
These simple songs of love and death ring true
In an age when we're afraid to show the heart –
'Whatever you say, say nothing', this in lieu
Of a creed that years ago joined prayer and art.
We say nothing and mean nothing now that we
Lose belief and, cynics in our loss,
Look down on the believer, this poetry –
The gospel of a soul that takes its cross,
Songs a life has earned or else are trash,
Salvation, suffered, sung by Johnny Cash.

Two Guitars

I. To My D-28

Your body's unblemished
And sweetly you're strung,
A beauty I dreamed of
Since I was young,
But I'm middle-aged
Losing hair, overweight,
And it's now you come to me,
My D-28.

As youngsters we dreamed
And talked of guitars,
We played out our crushes
On prized Yamahas,
And though we made music
When out on a date,
We wished we were playing
A D-28.

We played Epiphones, Yamahas,
Fenders – all good;
We played on them music
To suit every mood,
But deep down we dreamed

That sooner or late
We'd all find our very own
D-28.

The past becomes present,
The dream becomes true.
It was music I loved, dear
(I thought it was you);
You're all that I dreamed of
But now it's too late
For I'm pledged to another,
My D-28.

And still we make music
But now we both know
That there's no going back
To the long, long ago
For my road is taken,
I'm resigned to my fate,
My first and forever
D-28.

II. To My O-32

You are my Original,
Model 32,
There's no model on the catwalk
I'd swap, my love, for you;
Though others sing as sweetly
Inviting me to play,
It's you, my love, I'm stroking,
On you my head I lay.

How well we fit together,
My belly to your back,
I strum you with my fingers,
They slowly learn the knack
Of bringing forth your music
Caressing every string,
The bright notes of harmony
Between us as we sing.

The years we've been together,
The roads we've travelled. Yes!
There were times we made no music,
There were times of love's distress;
But come, love, let me hold you,
I look with eyes anew,

After all these years I know now
I want no love but you.

After all these years I know now
I want no love but you.

Double Portrait with a Painting by Chagall

'Double Portrait with a Wine Glass', Marc Chagall.
The coupling of true lovers in their bliss,
A song of songs of love before the Fall
More joyous than his portraits of a kiss.
The bird of love transports us here to see
This couple raise their wine glass once again;
We celebrate our anniversary,
The covenant I made on wedding Brenda,
Lovers as Chagall and Bella here
Floating in their love above their town.
Come to me and mount my shoulders, dear,
Come to me, an angel for your crown,
I bare my breast, support you. Have no fear.
When the wine is drained I'll lightly set you down.

The White Shirt

I bought a white shirt in *John's Menswear* today,
A sign that my youth is passing away –
A colour I once was unwilling to wear
When I had no belly and twice as much hair.

My reds and my yellows now blend into white,
My white shirt reflects all the colours of light
As I broaden my spectrum with each passing day,
My teeth getting longer, my hair turning grey.

Laughing at wisdom, youth boasts it's no more
Than energy ebbing. At full flow before
My colours reflected but aspects of white,
What vision I had dividing the light.

I'm free from the passions of uncertain youth –
I'm here at John Sexton's to buy me a suit;
I'll dress as I am with a collar and tie
And welcome the man. Farewell to the boy.

Farewell to the boy and welcome my prime
When my life and my love come together and rhyme
And all the old conflicts and all the old hurt
Surrender themselves in the sign of this shirt.

Elegy for a Drink Driver

There's one law for the city
And another law for us;
There's no taxi in our village,
We never see a bus.

I live alone, a bachelor,
I drive an ancient car,
So as not to be all night alone
I drive to Kincaid's bar

Where I drink a pint, a whiskey
And light up for a smoke,
I don't drink too much or smoke too much –
That way I'd be broke.

I'm a pensioned-off small farmer
Three miles from the bar,
I'm too old to walk there,
I have to take my car.

The guards have never stopped me
Driving home at night –
Despite the law, the local guards
Take pity on my plight.

A pint or two, a whiskey
And I'm off the road
If any guard should bag me
By that city-serving code

With its taxis, trains and buses
But how can I get home? –
The only other choice I have
Is to drink at home alone.

And I won't do that – it's not for drink
I go to Kincaid's bar
But to meet my friends for a chat and smoke
And share a joke and jar.

The law is for the city.
I break it – I've no choice;
There's no votes in speaking up for me:
My kind has no voice.

Pensioned-off, my Ireland
Is consigned to history;
Some day I'll run out of luck
And that's the end of me.

In The Silver Dollar

The Silver Dollar, a Country 'n' Western pub
Where one-man-bands twang out their nasal tat
For drinkers who don't listen, but here's the rub –
The barmaid's frank admission tells me that
If there's music no one listens, alas; and yet
If there's no music no one comes in at all
While, clustered under a massive TV set,
Football junkies watch the day's football.
One quiet night in the Dollar, old John Long,
Indigenous as Guinness, is ignored
As he sings his lusty local songs
While an exile on vacation videos.
He shows it on the telly when he's done
Where the drinkers watch the singer they've just shunned.

His Last Pint

He came into the village one last time
Defying cancer by an act of will
As he came into the village in his prime.

He left with me as his clock began to chime
Nine o'clock; swallowing a pill,
He came into the village one last time.

We stopped at Kincaid's bar; he couldn't climb
Out of my car until I helped him. Still,
As he came into the village in his prime,

He walked in unsupported, and I'm
Certain that the drinkers felt a chill
As he came into the village one last time.

He called for a Carlsberg and lime
Too weak now for the Guinness that he'd swill
When he came into the village in his prime.

But the cancer couldn't take his state of mind:
From the tap of life the dying drank his fill –
He came into the village one last time
As he came into the village in his prime.

The Maid behind the Bar

for Betty G.

'I'm sorry I can't serve you'
Hits him like a smack;
He wants another whiskey.
He's completely taken aback.

'You mean you're not serving me?'
'I'm sorry' the reply;
She empties, wipes his ashtray.
This stetsoned, moustached guy

Takes his money from the counter,
No questioning her rule
(All he's done is boast a bit),
Gets down from his stool,

The kind of guy who'd hit you
If you crossed him on the street
Leaves the bar this instant
Admitting his defeat.

God! the power of barmaids,
They make small boys of men –
The louder they are, the smaller,
And they'll come back again

In a week, a month, a season
To be forgiven and served again.
God! the power of barmaids,
They make small boys of men.

The Queen of Saturday Night

She's singing for her supper,
The queen of Saturday night –
'A one-man-band' they call her
Not knowing how they're right.

Her husband is her roadie,
He keeps an eye on her –
An unofficial bouncer
Backside to the bar.

It's bought them carpets, curtains,
Armchairs and settee,
A brand new fitted kitchen,
The latest gadgetry.

She cleans, she dusts, she polishes,
She irons all his shirts,
But come around the weekend
It's heels and mini-skirts.

For a few hours after *Newstime*
She's every inch the star
As she coaxes out the dancers
From the dart-board and the bar.

The Boghole Boys

The Boghole Boys in Kincaid's, Saturday nights,
A plain man's pub of polkas, jigs and reels,
See the neighbours sing and dance and fight
As they down their porter and kick up their heels.
The Boghole Boys are banjo, box, guitar
And anyone who cares to play along,
The Boghole Boys are the soul of such a bar,
The Boghole Boys are an afterhours of song.

The Boghole Boys in the Sunday morning choir,
Voices hoarse from last night's hooley, yet
They dose themselves with Strepsils, throats on fire
Their Sunday song's as good as you will get.
The Boghole Boys make music where they can
Keeping time when times no longer scan.

A Boghole Boy is Vindicated in his Local Pub

'You changes us when you comes in here.
There's times when only for this place
I'd go mad.'

Mountain Singer

Your very own laughed at you,
They didn't want to hear
The mountain you remembered
Because they were so near

The poverty and hunger
This country left behind
And the truth that you were singing
Could only remind

Them of an Ireland
Of which they were ashamed
So they dressed it up in shamrock
Forgetting whence they came.

They laughed at your singing
And even those who knew
The soul they were betraying
Turned their backs on you

And sanitised your music
For the concert hall
But they knew the mountain
Could outsing them all,

That, for all their fame and fortune,
Their dressed-up music palls
Before your rude, raw singing
For you outsang them all.

In the Gaeltacht

I. In *Óstán Oileán Acla*, July 2003

The *spéirbhean* is a drunkard
Today on Achill Sound –
The odd one speaking Irish,
English all around.

The *spéirbhean* is that drunkard
Who, leaving, waves at me
(The only one who's looking)
And staggers towards the sea.

Gaeltacht: an Irish speaking district; the state of being Irish.
Óstán Oileán Acla: literally, the Achill Island Hotel.
spéirbhean: in the aisling (vision) poems of the eighteenth century, the spéirbhean or 'vision-woman' is Ireland

II. In a *Gaeltacht* Pub

'*Pionnta* Guinness,' he asks the barman for a Guinness;
'And what are you having?' he turns and asks his wife.
'Water,' she replies – '*Uisce, más é do thoil é*'
(To the barman); 'Tap or bottle?' he replies
Whose English is fluent as his Irish
But the die-hard at the counter will insist
On speaking English to his wife and then translating
Into Irish for the barman. A crank gets pissed
Off with this purist at the counter
With his Irish-English-Irish; he explodes –
'We call a pint a *piúnt* here in the *Gaeltacht*
And you're a fucking teacher I suppose.'
So the barman serves in Irish when it's spoken
And to English, French and Germans while he who
Translates his wife for a glass of sparkling water
Must piss beneath a GENTS sign in the loo.

Pionnta Guinness: a pint of Guinness.
Uisce, más é do thoil é: water, please.

The Village Schoolmaster

I. Among Schoolchildren

These children here in front of me are ... what?
Neighbours' sons and daughters sent to school,
Little friends who heed me, sometimes not,
Who, years hence, might join me on a stool
In the local pubs as I grow old:
One by one, they'll saunter to the bar;
Now and then the odd one will make bold
As young bucks flaunt their manhood, jar by jar.

These children here in front of me are good,
They're all that I could hope for in the young,
They'll serve their parish well in adulthood
(The kind of thing that often goes unsung),
And some will leave, and some, perhaps, will find
That greater place – the parish of the mind.

II. The Road to Damascus

She looks me squarely in the eye
And says (no trace of fright),
'You think you're the biggest man in the world',
And, to my shame, she's right.

I persecute with learning,
Make her, and others, fail
In the name of education.
It's I, not she, who've failed.

This, then, is the moment,
Struck from my high horse,
I see the child before me –
Child most wondrous.

She looks at me, offended,
Her accusation mild.
Who would become a teacher
Must first become a child.

III. The Lone Star Trail

for Gerard Quinn

It started as a song –
A simple round
Of cowboys and of cattle

Till sound possessed the children
Who yelled
And neighed
And mooed:

Cowboy was a horse
And both were cattle.

Then the song became their pictures
Swift and rude.

They offer me their pictures for approval
(All suns and no horizons) …

I approve.

IV. The Hurt Bird

After playtime
Huddled in the classroom ...

In the yard
Jackdaws peck the ice
While the class guesses
The black birds:

Blackbirds?
(Laughter).

Crows?
Well yes ...
But jackdaws.
Those are jackdaws.
Why do they peck the ice?

Wonder
Becomes jackdaws' eyes
Rummaging the ice

Till suddenly
At the window opposite

– Oh the bird!
The poor bird!

At the shout
The jackdaws fright.

Sir, a robin sir ...
He struck the window
And he fell
And now he's dying
With his legs up
On the ice:

The jackdaws
Will attack it sir,

They will rip its puddings out.

I take the wounded bird,
Deadweight
In my open palm

– No flutter
No escaping

And lay it on the floor near heat,
The deadweight

Of the wound
Upon my coat.

Grasping
The ways of pain,
The pain of birds
They cannot name,
The class are curious
But quiet:

They will not frighten
The struggle
Of death and living.

Please sir,
Will he die?

And I
Cannot reply.

Alone
With utter pain

Eyes closed

The little body
Puffed and gasping

Lopsided
Yet upright:

He's alive,
The children whisper
Excited
As if witnessing
His birth.

Would he drink water sir?
Would he eat bread?
Should we feed him?

Lopsided
The hurt bird
With one eye open
To the world
Shits;

He moves
And stumbles.

I move
To the hurt bird:

The beak opens
– For food
Or fight?

I touch
The puffed red breast
With trepid finger;

I spoon water
To the throat:

It splutters.

Children crumb their lunches
Pleading to lay the broken bread
Within reach of the black head.

The bird
Too hurt to feed
Falls in the valley
Of the coat,
And as I help
It claws
And perches on my finger
Bridging the great divide
Of man and bird.

He hops
From my finger
To the floor

And flutters
Under tables
Under chairs

Till exhausted
He tucks his head
Between wing and breast
Private
Between coat and wall.

The class
Delights in silence
At the sleeping bird.

The bird sir …
What is it –
A robin?
– Look at the red breast.

But you never see a robin
With a black head.

I tell them
It's a bullfinch
Explaining the colours why:

I answer their questions

From the library.

And the children draw the bullfinch

– With hurt
And gasp
And life

With the fearlessness of pain
Where the bird will fright

And in the children's pictures
Even black and grey
Are bright.

V. Getting to Know You

Thomas,
You don't trust me –
I can tell from your trapped eyes.
How can I help you,
My sulky friend?
Tell you I love you?
(That would seem like lies).
To reach out to touch you
Might offend.

Give you your head;
Watch over
In so far as any human can;
Coax you with tacit kindness;
Greet you, man to man ...

Yes, Thomas,
I am strong
(But equal) –
And, Thomas,
We are both 'at school':
Both circling round
A common understanding,
Both sniffing at the smile

That sweetens rules.

Today you bounce up to me,
Your eyes the rising sun:

We share your secret story –

Hello!
God bless you,
Tom …

VI. Primary Education

He put on the blues this morning,
Blue shirt, v-neck, blue tie –
The stamp of conformity.
His own clothes would defy

The system we impose on him –
He can't wear what he will:
How different is a uniform
To our desire to kill

The little spark of genius
That makes us different?
In my schooldays, I remember,
Everybody went

Dressed as they had clothes to wear –
Those of us with shoes
And underpants were 'sissies';
If we could, we'd choose

The bare feet, short pants, no 'knickers'
Of the jealous tots-to-twelves
For freedom isn't granted.
We win it from ourselves.

VII. The Interview

'How would you sell yourself as a teacher?'
What can I say but a teacher's not for sale,
That our choice of word often will betray us;
She's interested, but I can see I've failed

To convince her of the value of this reading,
That, a teacher, I'm bound to pass along
The values inherent in our language,
Values I'd inculcate in the young.

I could if I would blow my own trumpet,
Dazzle with achievement – then she'd see
What selling is, and all of pence and ha'pence,
But I'm suspicious she's not opened my CV.

This, then, is the system that I work for –
Blessed are the glib for they shall gain;
'What profit it a man to gain the world ...'
I whisper to myself to keep me sane.

VIII. A Teacher Sings the Blues

I've never found the time
To indulge the child within –
All day I'm teaching children.
There are times I could give in

It's so lonely in the classroom,
And the kids don't understand
That I, too, hurt like they do;
And my! how kids can wound.

At lunch time I'm 'on duty',
I patrol the shrill school-yard
A sandwich and a cuppa
In my hand. Oh, it's so hard

To keep an eye on children,
And if one of them gets hurt
You wonder if they'll sue you
And you've never been in court.

And the kids are getting bolder
And you know this could be good
Because, a child, you'd no such freedom,
You did as you were told.

And when you retire on pension
With forty years put in
They'll make a presentation
In the local *Arms* or *Inn*;

And you'll look back, if you're lucky,
On a job, you hope, well done.
Then shortly you're forgotten –
You know that life moves on.

IX. Death of a Teacher

The most public man in the village,
A teacher performs, is on view;
At fifty, he cannot continue.
Alas, what else can he do?

Fifteen more years to retirement
And half pay the rest of his life,
His kids have ambitions for college
And he won't make a slave of his wife.

So he stands there alone in the classroom
Too shrivelled and dry to shed tears,
Alone in a riot of children
He clocks in the days and the years.

And the children grow up, leave the village,
The world is theirs while he stays,
Trapped in a vision that's crumbling
He lives out the rest of his days.

Trapped in a vision that's crumbling
He lives out the rest of his days.

X. On the Death of a Pupil

The requiem ends through children's happy cries –
It's playtime in the yard in his old school:
No one who's a child thinks they will die,
It takes a while to learn that life's this cruel.
The children playing football play their game,
More gape at the coffin from the wall;
In his thirties, the kids don't know his name
But I remember him, remember all –
The years he spent before me, a young boy,
A young life cancelled pointlessly by chance.
You don't expect to see your pupils die.
No doubt someone's said we should give thanks
For the life he lived, the good that he achieved –
Clichés that we need, are half believed.

XI. The Teacher

for David Mason

I wish away my life until the pension
Hoping that, just once, I will connect
With sympathy that is beyond attention;
Instead I keep good order, earn respect.
Once I had a vision for my village –
I'd bring to it a gift of poetry;
Tonight the talk's of quotas and of tillage
And how the barmaid gives out beer for free.
And yet, I've not lost hope in my own people –
My vision was at fault; these people need
To sing and dance, get drunk below the steeple
That accuses them of gossip and of greed.
I mind their children, give them right of way
Into a world I've seen and try to say.

XII. Geography Lesson

'What are the four directions?'
They all know what I'm at;
Not Tom – he goes his own way
('Right, Left, First and Last').

And which is the right answer –
North, South, East and West?
Fine if that's where you want to go
But for Tom, his way is best.

Right and Left and First and Last –
That's the way he goes;
North and South and East and West
Are only for those

Who travel by the compass,
But a compass has no place
In Right and Left and First and Last,
In what he has to face.

Right and Left and First and Last,
He'll make his way along
With North and South and East and West
To where neither answer's wrong.

XIII. Clearing Out His Classroom, a Teacher Gives an Old Globe to a Child

The world has changed since first I got this globe,
The map has changed, the climate even more;
Man's walked on the moon, and now we probe
Further space and plumb the planet's core.
The atom split, we split now, lobe by lobe,
The human being, desperate to explore
Ourselves, our world. In more sober
Times we lived without such answers. Sure
Times have changed; the world that old globe shows
Is kaput as ancient Egypt, Greece or Rome;
Nonetheless, for all the new world knows,
It's still looking for the word that makes it home.
You take this battered globe as though 'twere new:
The world is in your hands, depends on you.

XIV. On Being Appointed Principal Teacher of Moyvane National School

For my people who walked barefoot miles to school,
For the children in the years of hand-down dress,
For the hurt who can't forget being branded 'fool',
For the ones who left this parish to success;
For the youths that died in foreign wars who fought
When adopted lands conscripted them, and those
Who lived and died for Ireland, those who wrought
A nation from a peasant's ragged clothes;
For those who perished homeless, those who took
Their lives in desperation, and for all
Who were wronged or felt diminished by the book,
For those who heard and followed its great call;
For all my predecessors have set free
From the days of the hedge-school down to me,
I accept this post.

Keeper of the Story

for Dick Spring

I. To Pádraig Pearse

for Declan Kiberd

I see you, Pearse, in Dublin with your sword –
Cuchulainn (hardly!), a poser with a dream.
In the new state, our teachers often bored
Us pink with *'Ireland – How She'd Seem*
To Pádraig Pearse'. I didn't give a damn –
Those essays were for old men to off-load
Their hang-ups at new freedom. Pearse the man
Was never taught us – teachers toed
The party line in everything they taught;
A poet like Pearse was dangerous, and so
They cast him as our conscience, and some bought
It. I didn't want to know.
They forged you in their image, and I sought
A way to write those essays and to grow.

Pádraig Pearse: Patrick Henry Pearse, poet and teacher, an executed leader of the 1916 Easter Rising which led to the foundation of the Irish Republic

II. Knocklong

Oh, take me through the byroads
To those places named in song:
Along the road less travelled
Is the station of Knocklong
Where shots rang out for freedom
In nineteen and nineteen
With young Seán Hogan rescued
By Seán Treacy and Dan Breen.

As I drive to Tipperary
I recall the lore,
The War of Independence –
Here I park my car
On a road become a songline
And walk into the song
'The Rescue of Seán Hogan
At the Station of Knocklong'.

The station's now deserted,
Blocked up, overgrown
But not the gallous story,
An empire overthrown;
But I am overtaken
By the traffic on the road

Who hoot at this obstruction,
The progress I have slowed.

And so I take the burden
Of history and drive
Into Tipperary
Where I see New Ireland thrive;
But I'm glad I took the byroad
That led me into song –
Many roads to Tipperary.
Only one Knocklong.

Gallous: a composite word incorporating gallant, callous and gallows

III. Dan Breen
for Fintan O'Toole

'There's a great gap between a gallous story and a dirty deed' – The Playboy of the Western World

My *Fight for Irish Freedom* by Dan Breen –
I read it like a western; I'd pretend
To be a freedom fighter at thirteen –
It made a change from 'Cowboys'; I'd spend
My spare time freeing Ireland in my head
Reliving his adventures one by one –
The policemen that he shot at Solohead,
Romance about the days spent on the run.

A nation born of romance and of blood,
Once ruled by men who killed for their beliefs,
Now a nation grown to adulthood
Losing faith in heroes, tribal chiefs.
Dan Breen is laid with the giants who held sway;
The gallous reads of dirty deeds today.

IV. Two Brothers

Two brothers joined the column
To fight for *Ireland Free*,
Then the Treaty divided them;
The story that united
Shattered with the dream:
A man without a story
Is a man who must redeem himself.
The community of purpose
Shattered like a glass,
Each seeing his own image
Singly, piece by piece
Where once all life was mirrored;
He would again be whole –
Fighting for their stories,
Comrades, brothers, soldiers
Join in Civil War
And so did these two brothers.
They never again shared
Sleep beneath the same roof,
A pint in any bar,
Dinner at one table.
And so, the fighting over,
They both moved to the Bronx,

Married, raised families –
Never once
Did they communicate.
I remember as a child
Their (separate) summer visits,
Two storied men who smiled at me
And played my childish games:
I remember with affection,
At times recite their names
When opposite *is* opposite.
Some things won't unite:
Wounds will knit, not stories
Till the poetry is right.

Column: i.e. Flying Column, an active service unit of the IRA during the Irish War of Independence (1919–21)

V. A Windfall

The castle – Anglo-Irish – where the knights
Held out despite the English through the years;
They fought, and, when it made no sense to fight,
Turned Protestant like many of their peers.
The Civil War. In 'twenty-two, the knight's
An enemy of the people (so they say).
Some hotheads want to burn him out; one night
He's raided by the local IRA.
The old knight in his wheelchair holds his ground –
If they burn the castle, they must burn him too;
They won't kill him; they put their petrol down
And head back to the local to review
The situation. They don't return. (They're jarred.)
The knight retains their petrol for his yard.

VI. The Mother

Forced to view his body –
Her guerrilla son
Shot dead in an ambush
By an occupier's gun;

Forced to view his body
In the workhouse where,
Lest there should be reprisals,
She could show no mother's care;

Forced to view his body,
She denied she knew her son
Then left him to an unmarked grave.
That's how the war was won.

VII. What the Provo Said to Me
Easter 2003

It was a true Republican
I met that Easter day,
One who knew his history
And was not afraid to say

That the time for war was over,
That the end had come,
That, short of hitting London
With a nuclear bomb,

The time for war was over
Except for a die-hard few
But that loudest against the ceasefire
Were a cowardly crew

Who suddenly were brave men
When the war was won
All huff and puff and posture
Who never fired a gun,

All mouth against the ceasefire,
Hangers-on he'd dub
'Fuckers who did nothing,
Patriots of the pub,

While others did the fighting
When fighting was required,
I tell them when I see them
They were always on ceasefire;

I tell those cowardly fuckers
They were always on ceasefire.'

VIII. Up the Republic!

No one listened to us
When we sang contemporary
So we changed to rebel ballads
And shamrock *graw-machree.*

We sing for local drinkers
Who cheer and dance and shout
And call the English 'bastards'
When whiskey, lager, stout

Have made them bar-room patriots;
We sing for Yankees too
Who, thinking that it's Irish,
Ask for 'Toor-

a-loor-a-loor-al',
That Tin Pan Alley song:
We Blarney-and-Killarney
Till the whole place sways along.

We could be singing better
(The stuff we used to sing)
But shut-eyed introspection
Won't make the rafters ring.

So it's bawl those rebel ballads
And every kind of shite
As we die for Ireland
Twenty times a night.

It's bawl those rebel ballads
Each night from half past ten,
The sound check done till the clock strikes one
We're die-for-Ireland men.

Up the Republic!

IX. On Being Refused Publication in *The Spectator*

My poems don't cross the borders of his land:
The editor's enjoyed them, but he writes
That the readers of his mag won't understand
So he's keeping these 'fine poems' out of sight.
My poems address my nation is his plea –
'Do they reach across the borders and address
The English who don't know your history?'
(Whose conquest left my country in a mess).
'You obviously have,' he tells me, 'the right stuff
So I hope you'll send us some more poems anon';
As if he's not already said enough,
He holds my poems to show them to his Mum
Who's Irish, wed a Welshman – to my dismay
'But they split up,' he quips, 'so it's OK.'

X. Galvin and Vicars

in memoriam Mick Galvin, killed in action, Kilmorna, Knockanure (in the parish of Newtown Sandes, now Moyvane) on Thursday, 7 April 1921; and Sir Arthur Vicars, shot at Kilmorna House, his residence, on Thursday, 14 April 1921.

Mick Galvin, Republican,
Arthur Vicars, who knows what?
– Some sort of Loyalist –
In Ireland's name were shot:

Vicars by Republicans,
Galvin by the *Tans*,
Both part of my history –
The parish of Newtown Sandes

Named to flatter landlords
(But 'Moyvane' today,
Though some still call it 'Newtown' –
Some things don't go away

Easily). Galvin and Vicars,
I imagine you as one –
Obverse and reverse
Sundered by the gun.

History demands
We admit each other's wrongs:
Galvin and Vicars,
Joined only in this song,

Nonetheless I join you
In the freedom of this state
For art discovers symmetries
Where politics must wait.

Tans: i.e. Black and Tans, a unit of the crown forces during the Irish War of Independence

XI. On the Execution by the Irish Free State of Four Republican Soldiers at Drumboe, Co. Donegal, 14 March 1923

The letter of Lieutenant Timothy O'Sullivan to his mother on the eve of his execution

Drumboe Castle,
Stranorlar,
Donegal.
13.3.1923.

Dear mother,

At 4 o'clock this evening
It was announced that I
With three others of my comrades
Tomorrow morning die.

It wasn't unexpected,
Let God's will be done;
I wouldn't change places
Now with anyone.

In Donegal they've offered masses
To prepare us for this day,

We made a general confession
To Fr McMullen of Ballybofey;

The priest took our addresses
And will write to you,
We'll have mass tomorrow morning,
Holy communion too.

Dear mother, don't be troubled,
Let no trace of sadness lurk
For I'm sure that God will judge us
According to our works.

I'll wear your beads tomorrow,
They'll be sent you with my clothes.
Goodbye again, God bless you
And my dear friends in Listowel.

My comrades send best wishes,
We all are treated well.
I forgive our executioners.
Mother dear, farewell.

Your fond son,
Timmy.

XII. The Guardian of the Dead

Keeper of the story
And guardian of the dead
(Soldiers of the Republic
'Executed'

By the Black and Tans –
'Murdered' is what he'd say),
He tends the roadside monuments
Of the fallen IRA

(The men of the Flying Columns
Of 1921,
Locals who, but for history,
Would have taken up no gun),

A man who's out of fashion,
A man who'll not be led;
Alone at the roadside monuments
He minds his dead.

That's Football!

for Mick O'Connell

I. At the Ball Game

for Seamus Heaney

Everything out there you see
Is a version of reality
As heroes triumph over doubt
And bring their kind of truth about.

Each, according to his way,
Engages on the field of play,
And, urging on, the faithful crowd
Are cheering, praising, cursing loud
For beauty only will suffice,
Beauty to infuse our lives:
No cup, no trophy will redeem
Victory by ignoble means.

And, so, we take the field today
To find ourselves in how we play,
Out there on the field to be
Ourselves, a team, where all can see;
For nothing is but is revealed
And tested on the football field.

II. Munster Football Final, 1924

Nothing polarises like a war,
And, of all wars, a civil war is worst;
It takes a century to heal the scars
And even then some names remain accursed.
The tragedies of Kerry, open wounds –
John Joe Sheehy on the run in 'twenty-four,
The Munster Final in the Gaelic Grounds:
There's something more important here than war.
John Joe Sheehy, centre forward, Republican,
Con Brosnan, Free State captain, centrefield;
For what they love, they both put down the gun –
On Con's safe conduct, Sheehy takes the field.
In an hour the Kerry team will win.
Sheehy will vanish, on Brosnan's bond, again.

III. The Team of 'Sixty-Two

for Garry McMahon

No logo here on jersey, togs or boot,
A team who played for pure love of a game
That reveals its players in their truth,
A team that asked no money, handled fame.
We got a lift to the wonder of TV,
To a distant village, a small set in the hall,
We paid like all the others just to see
Our team's ascent to glory raise us all.
For we believed in heroes way back then
Who raised themselves to immortality;
Before me in that photo, fifteen men
Who from my youth were more than men to me.
That picture hangs where once a saint or pope
Would look down from the wall in pious hope.

IV. A Footballer

He could have played with better
But he chose his own;
Playing with his county
He'd never carry home

The trophy all aspire to
But that's not why he played:
If he played with another county
He'd feel he had betrayed

Himself, his art, his people,
So he plays out his career
Away from the glare of headlines.
And yet sometimes you'll hear

From followers of football
The mention of his name.
It's enough that they believe in him,
His way, his truth, his game.

V. The Game of Your Life
for Bernard O'Donoghue

Whatever way it's kicked out, face the ball!
While wingers await delivery in space,
Centrefield must rise above the maul
And safely field, taking thought to place
The ball of fortune with the chosen one
And will him on to make the greatest use
Of what he's given: the ball passed on,
He solos towards the goal as play ensues.
For now's the time when great men must redeem
The story of the game from death, defeat:
The game of life's the story of a team
Who cannot rest until their task's complete –
To take the cup, the cup that cannot pass
And raise it up in glory for the mass.

VI. Dancing Through
homage to Mikey Sheehy, footballer

Nureyev with a football,
You solo to the goal
Where the swell of expectation
Spurts in vain –
O master of the ritual,
O flesh of tribal soul,
Let beauty be at last
Released from pain ...

Now grace eludes its marker
Creating its own space
While grim defenders
Flounder in its wake;
And the ball you won from conflict
Yields to your embrace –
Goal beckons like a promise ...
And you take.

For Eamon Lloyd

When Munster played the Tigers, Welford Road
Was the land of heart's desire for every fan;
Match tickets were more valuable than gold.
I travelled ticketless with my teenage son
Just to be there in Leicester on the day
With Munster men and women for the game –
To find a likely pub and watch the play
Was as much as we could hope for until Eamon
Lloyd with whom we stayed, a Tigers' fan,
Gave my son his season ticket for the match,
What money couldn't buy, this kindest man
Gave John his heart's desire. Old friend, we watched
The game on television. And Munster won.
'Twas nothing to your kindness to my son.

Local Hero, International Star

He was a county minor,
Played midfield but was slow,
Won an All-Ireland medal
But was smart enough to know

He'd not make it playing Gaelic
So he switched to rugby and
Became an international hero
Playing for Ireland.

Playing Gaelic football's
Not too lucrative,
The rugby network
Had more to give,
Now instead of commercial travelling
He's an executive.

At the famous playwright's funeral
The papers all were there
Noting the famous faces;
They noted this great player,

And in the queue I overheard
An old GAA man say
'If he was a small bit faster,
He'd be a poor man today.'

Dainty Man

winner of Ireland's first coursing Derby, 1930

The village blacksmith in his forge
Breathes the whole day long
Soot and smoke enough to choke
The man but not his song,

The song that takes him from his forge
To that Derby day
When *Dainty Man*, his hound, outran
Ireland's best greyhounds;

And how, the coursing over
And money sought to buy
Dainty Man, his owner
Steady in his joy

Refused the rich man's offer,
Faced his native bog
Saying, 'I've lived in poverty all my life
But I'll keep my dog.

Poem for Nessa, Five Years Old

She brings me a pale strawberry
While I'm sitting on the loo,
The last one in the garden,
Says, 'Dad, this is for you.'

I don't know what I'd do without her –
There simply is no place
That she won't come and find me,
A smile upon her face.

For Nessa always finds things –
No matter what is lost,
Nessa's sure to find it.
She's found me in the past

When I've been lost and lonely,
Nowhere to lay my head,
She's brought me hope – like strawberries.
Who cares if they're not red!

Poem for John

A bucket on his head, a pretend soldier
Wearing Mammy's boots that reached above his knee …
He remembers this quite clearly now he's older –
The magic world he lived in, turning three.
He'd go to bed sitting on my shoulder,
His *Daddy Doodle*, oh so proud of me!:
It's not that what's between us has grown colder –
To grow apart is part of being free.

I love you, son, as on the day you came
Into my life, a baby who would need
All I could give, my love, a home, a name,
My word made flesh though not born of my seed.
Tonight you put your Teddy from your bed –
The magic wanes, the world looms ahead.

Table Quiz

The questions come out neatly one by one.
Son, each one has an answer that's precise;
No room for thinking here as, like a gun,
The mind fires out the answers. Here a voice
Whispers loud its knowledge like a boast,
All that can be known for certain's here:
There are winners, there are losers as we toast
A world where each question's answered clear,
A world where simplicity prevails.
Outside this circle nothing's answered thus,
This futile show of certainty that fails
Every decent question asked of us.
So spit out all the answers while you can
Before the questions come that make a man.

Sick Child

He's too young to suffer, Lord, like this;
Take this burden from him, make it mine:
I've long put up with troubles; the abyss
I've long looked into. In denying
Whatever it's that troubles him, he pales
And pukes with what the secret won't admit;
Everything the doctors give him fails –
Is there nothing those doctors have can hit
The cause of his strange sickness and can cure
Whatever it is that troubles him this while?
I'd prefer to suffer than endure
Helpless while he suffers. He's my child.
Take this burden from him, hear my plea.
Let me take his load that it unburden me.

Grandad

You lived for him, his grandad, day by day;
He kept you young – the villagers guessed right:
At eighty years you still had strength to play,
And he'd stay with you (his big treat) Friday nights.
He followed you wherever you would go,
You flew to England (his first time on a plane);
You were his Christmas morning, his fall of snow;
He'd as soon be with his grandad as at home.

A widower, all you asked of life
Was to see how he got on when he grew up;
You're buried with my mother ('Grandad's wife');
You kept her grave; now he and I keep up
Your grave. He's got your feeling for the task,
Growing into all for which you'd ask.

A Widower

They thought to make you marry when she died;
Accounts of matches came from women who
Would share your life should you take one as bride,
But, constant as your love for her was true,
You lived alone for nearly thirty years
In the home you made with Mam, an invalid.
I remember once you told me over beers
The reason why you did the things you did.
You said you'd bring no other to your life
Fearing I, your only child, would be upset.
Not so, Dad: caring for your wife
You knew the love that lovers don't forget.
The others who would wed you came too late.
A love like yours would take no other mate.

Granada

My mother should have been here, but ill health
Confined her to her bed much of her life –
That, and her lack of worldly wealth,
Her meagre store, a village grocer's wife.
She'd read about it when she'd sight to read,
Heard it sung (in English) on LP;
Confined to bed, her mind was all she'd need –
To see it in the flesh she left to me.
Enough for her that she had heard its song;
Enough for her that, though she'd never see
Granada and all for which she longed,
Enough it was to know their poetry.
Through narrow streets, among the souvenirs,
I think of her through mingled sweat and tears.

Nerja

There are fewer to send postcards to at home,
My people have all but disappeared,
No one to call up on the phone,
No one to worry about over here.
I sit in my apartment looking out
On *Mare Nostrum* but that sea's not mine,
This beaker full of the warm south,
The sun, flamenco and the Spanish wine.
Parents play with children in the pool,
The sun blasts down on pale skins oiled-to-tan,
Here on the balcony it's cool
As the hottest it ever gets to in Moyvane.
And there's no one I need call now on the phone:
The dead have taken with them much of home.

Home

My family are dying one by one,
My uncles and my aunts – just Peg now left:
The ones who, returning to Moyvane,
Brought England with them in the way they dressed.
They'd travel home from Shannon on the bus
(We'd no cars back then to make the trip),
Though a lifetime 'over', they spoke the same as us,
Still the same old Kerry accent rough and rich.
They never lost their Kerry: they'd no need
To lose themselves in England, or to pine
For Ireland lost as they passed on their seed;
My cousins are English, and our line
Still comes home to visit: they belong,
A people and a place that still are one.

The Fitzs Come to Town

Those sultry summer nights in Dinny Mack's,
The Fitzs home from England; the whole clan
Singing, dancing, drinking for the crack.
Those nights were the talk of half Moyvane.
Musicians came and played till closing time,
The Fitzs danced their old-time sets again,
Drink flowed like talk that's loosed by beer and wine
And teens accepted shandies from the men.
Those sultry summer nights in Dinny Mack's
All were welcome among the Fitzs who
Brought the summer with them and relaxed
Who never shirked when there was work to do.
And Dinny Mack would stand us the odd round
Saying "'Tis better than the Carnival
when the Fitzs come to town.'

Cutting Grass in Glenalappa

In the name of all who went before us we cut this grass:

The ones who farmed the homestead,
The rest who emigrated
To become firemen, policemen and domestics in New York,

Factory workers and navvies in London,
        Leicester, Sheffield, Saint Helen's,
Thelwall, Dagenham, Watford.
In your name we cut this grass.

Know today you're not forgotten
As my son and I cut the grass you cut before us
At home in Glenalappa.

In the name of your sons and daughters we cut this grass,
And their children
And their children's children;

And for the time when there's no Fitzmaurice
        left in Glenalappa,
When the family have scattered like seeds on the wind,
When all that's left here of the Fitzmaurices is green grass,

In the name of all those generations, today we
        cut this grass.

For the Fitzmaurices of Glenalappa

Nesta,
'Brood mare of the Geraldines',
Is where we began:

For six hundred years
Fitzmaurices, Fitzgeralds –
Nesta's clan,
Builders of abbeys
And castles,
Connoisseurs of poetry,
Horses and fine wine,
Were conquerors of the land.

But the Fitzmaurices,
Normans,
Had become 'more Irish than the Irish'
As time went on.

Our castles fell to Elizabeth,
The Lords of Kerry fell
(Except those who submitted
To England's will –
They kept their lands).

The builders of abbeys and castles
Are found in Kerry still
In small holdings
In glens like Glenalappa,
My ancestral home.
I travelled there this Christmas
With my son.

*

My father,
His father
And his father's father
Sat around the fire
At Christmas
In Glenalappa.

As I did.

The fire is out
This Christmas,
The house deserted,
No Fitzmaurice now
In Glenalappa.

Farewell
All the Toms, Dicks, Jacks,

Noras, Ellens, Margarets
In every generation
Who sat around the fire
In Glenalappa.

Where are you, this Christmas,
My people?

Everywhere but in Glenalappa.

And somewhere in New York,
First cousins I've never met,
Whose names I don't even know.

For all the fires that burned
At Christmas in Glenalappa,
For all the generations
Who sat around that fire,
For all my people,
Dead, alive or yet to be born
For whom this place is home,
Out of our history
I make this poem.

Fitzmaurice of Glenalappa.

ACKNOWLEDGEMENTS

Several of these poems were first published in: *An Ríocht*, *Chapman* (Scotland), *Cúm*, *Heart of Kerry*, *Poetry Ireland Review*, *Quadrant* (Australia), *The Clifden Anthology*, *The Evansville Review* (USA), *The Kerryman*, *The Lyric* (USA), *The North Kerry Championship Senior Football Final Programmes* 2002, 2003, THE SHO*p*, *The Stony Thursday Book*.

Some were broadcast on TG4 (*Coinne le Gabriel Fitzmaurice*), RTÉ Radio 1 (*The Arts Show*, *Bowman Saturday*, *The Enchanted Way*) and on Radio Kerry.

'The Day Christ Came to Moyvane' was published in *Human Rights Have No Borders: Voices of Irish Poets* (Marino Books, 1998).

'On Being Appointed Principal Teacher of Moyvane National School' was published in *I Am of Kerry* (Currach Press, 2003).

'The Game of Your Life' was published (in an early version) in *Voices and Poetry of Ireland*

(HarperCollins, 2003) and read on the accompanying CD by Paul McGrath.

'*In Memoriam* John B. Keane' was published in *Come All Good Men and True: Essays from the John B. Keane Symposium* (Mercier Press, 2004) and in *John B. Keane, Playwright of the People* (North Kerry Literary Trust, 2004).

'A Footballer' and 'Local Hero, International Star' are published on the *Terrace Talk Ireland – Sports Poetry* website.

Also by Gabriel Fitzmaurice

POEMS FROM THE IRISH:
COLLECTED TRANSLATIONS

Old favourites and cutting-edge new poets sit easily together in this dual-language collection of Irish poetry from the seventeenth century to the present day.

1 86023 156 X

I AND THE VILLAGE

A superb collection of poetry in which Fitzmaurice explores the places and people around him to bring to light themes of universal importance.

1 86023 149 7